T0199030

Leah's GIFT

A Story about Reframing Loss

Balboa Press books may be ordered through booksellers or by contacting:

Balboa Press
A Division of Hay House
1663 Liberty Drive
Bloomington, IN 47403
www.balboapress.com
1 (877) 407-4847

ISBN: 978-1-9822-5058-4 (sc)
ISBN: 978-1-9822-5057-7 (e)

Library of Congress Control Number: 2020913063

Print information available on the last page.

Balboa Press rev. date: 08/19/2020

BALBOA.PRESS
A DIVISION OF HAY HOUSE

$\mathcal{A}$DVANCE PRAISE
FOR LEAH'S GIFT

This autobiographical account is a touching portrayal of a mother's loss.

The way Destanne combines her visual art and written words to express emotions was both evocative and compelling. I was driven to continue reading to the end.

I found these two sentences particularly moving:

"Spark of life is our mystery…. So is … [death]," and "I've never felt more alive in my grief."

Both these quotations eloquently express life's beauty and mystery. I'm sure her positive message will be an inspiration to many.

C. Bouchard, End of Life Doula/Educator

———————————

I never cease to be inspired by your courage and vulnerability to share your journey and your gifts.

Sharing in your loss and grief as a young woman ultimately taught me love and gratitude. It walked me through some hard days myself as a mother.

Thank you for opening your heart up so generously time and time again; you are changing lives every day, Destanne.

M. Sullivan, Dietitian

This book is so beautifully written.

I was especially impacted by the story of the ravens. I have never told anyone, but on the morning of June 13, I awoke to ravens cawing outside my bedroom at Tekarra [Lodge] at 5 a.m., and I knew it was connected to Leah. I had never heard them before. To this day, when I hear them, I am reminded of Leah.

I believe this [book] will help others; what you have brought together in finding meaning and healing is very powerful, and to be able to articulate it is a further gift."

C. Robb, Nurse

Leah's GIFT

A Story about Reframing Loss

Destanne Norris

For Tekarra, James, and Norman, with love.

Leah Marie Brown

December 1, 1993 – June 12, 1995

CONTENTS

Preface xi

Electrogenesis 1

Mother and Babe 1 4

Mother and Babe 2 9

Inner Landscapes 13

View from the Rock Gardens 17

Moments in Time 21

Awakening at the Site 25

Long Mornings 28

The Way We Were 31

Iris 37

Afterword 43

Acknowledgments 45

$\mathscr{L}$IST OF ARTWORKS

All measurements given in inches

Destanne Norris, *Electrogenesis*, 1985, oil on canvas, 66 x 48. Collection of the artist 1

Destanne Norris, *Mother and Babe 1*, 1986, graphite on paper, 2 x 2. Collection of the artist 4

Destanne Norris, *Mother and Babe 2*, 1986, photograph 17 x 15 from a slide of the original oil on canvas, 34 x 33. Collection of the artist 9

Destanne Norris, *Inner Landscapes 1 and 2*, 1985, graphite on paper, 18 x 24 each. Collection of the artist 13

Destanne Norris, *View from the Rock Gardens*, 1988, oil on canvas, 24 x 30. Collection of the artist 17

Destanne Norris, *Moments in Time 1 and 2*, 1995, pen and watercolor on paper, 8.5 x 11 each. Private Collection 21

Destanne Norris, *Awakening at the Site*, 1995, oil on canvas, 16 x 14. Collection of the artist 25

Destanne Norris, *Long Mornings*, 1996, graphite on paper, 6.5 x 10. Private Collection 28

Destanne Norris, *The Way We Were*, 1995, oil on canvas, 30 x 54. Collection of the artist 31

Destanne Norris, *Iris*, 1996, oil on canvas, 40 x 24. Private Collection 37

You would know the secret of death,

But how shall you find it unless you seek

it in the heart of life?

The owl whose night-bound eyes are

blind unto the day cannot unveil the mystery of light.

If you would indeed behold the spirit of death,

open your heart wide unto the body of life.

For life and death are one,

even as the river and sea are one.

—Kahlil Gibran, *The Prophet*

PREFACE

I am inviting you to share in my experience and to face the questions that tragedy and the loss of a loved one thrust upon us.

These questions are important as they help us to live as fully as we can, whether we have our own grief or not. They allow us to access the essence of our life, our meaning, and ultimately, our own death.

For those who've lost a loved one, you know how processing and moving through memories and sorrow are painful and difficult. One of the ways that helped me was to honor and celebrate my daughter Leah's life by having an art exhibition.

In structuring this written story, I've included each image of the artworks from this exhibition and used the title of each artwork as the chapter title. The order of the images and chapters is the order in which the artworks were exhibited.

While I am openly and transparently sharing my experience and what helped me, I am not promoting or advocating any one belief system or religion. The best I can do is to show and tell you my own personal journey. And if you're like me, you have questions. You want to know *why;* you want answers.

One of my greatest realizations was that I needed to reframe my questions.

When I did that, the answers came, and I knew what to do. This book, which has been waiting to be written for many years, is another one of those answers. It's my hope *Leah's Gift* inspires you.

ℰLECTROGENESIS

Electrogenesis (1985)

Electrogenesis. Is that even a word? I was contemplating my painting and wondering what it should be called when this word popped into my head. I heard, *Electrogenesis*. Nearly as fast as the word came to me, I found a dictionary, and much to my astonishment, there it was with the definition: "the production of electricity in the tissues of a living organism."

"Electrogenesis" became the title for my painting of a toddler joyfully splashing in the waters along the waterline, oblivious to what could be. Why had I painted a foreboding, unpredictable, midnight sky with the glowing, soft, yellow moon tucked behind the piercing, triangular shape alight in fiery reds slipping down from the heavens, reaching out to her through space? I made this painting in my second-year painting class at university in 1985. At that time, the sentimental subject matter was borderline acceptable, but to my relief, my professor nodded. He explained there was a mysterious edge to the painting that left the viewer unsure as to what was happening or *going to happen* to this young child immersed in its own world in the water.

Where had this image come from? Why was I attracted to painting a baby? I have no idea. At twenty-five years old, I was not even thinking about being a mother. The picture I'd used for reference was of a child dancing in a field of flowers. I'd explored some thoughts in several thumbnail graphite sketches in my drawing book before embarking on the final image. In each sketch, I had tried to capture the energy bursting out of this joyful child attempting to discover the right environment for her. Giving way to my intuition when starting to paint on the sixty-six-inch by forty-eight-inch canvas, none of my preliminary sketches resembled what became the final painting: "Electrogenesis." Its meaning remained a mystery to me until 1995, ten years later.

Recall came while I was curled up in a ball, writhing in agony, on the dank, spring earth at the picnic site not far from the rushing waters of the Maligne River. I saw mental flashes of the painting "Electrogenesis" and other paintings I had made, as well as things I wrote, did, and said, all before my daughter was born. They exploded in my mind's eye. Leah, our one-and-a-half-year-old daughter and youngest child, was missing.

Even before I looked up from my lawn chair to scour the tranquil scene before me, I had this feeling of dread. "Leah!" I hollered. "Where's Leah?" The world around me stopped turning. My entire being was sucked into a vacuum, and all that existed was finding Leah. Like a well-aimed bullet, I shot through the grasses and scrub to the low bank bordering the surging waters, all the while yelling—screaming—her name.

Leah loved the water. At two weeks old, we had started taking her to our local indoor pool, where the constant rumble and hum of the water slide would seem to soothe her while her siblings played in the kids' pool. And as soon as she was old enough to be in the water with us, she was splashing and frolicking in our arms with glee.

Now without a sound, she had disappeared from our sight. I thought her dad was watching her, and he thought I was. Her family, her nanny, and friends—we were all there. I saw nothing at the water's edge except the gentle eddy below my feet that left and then met up again with the fast-flowing river. Following the bank downstream, I ran to the Sixth Bridge, which crossed the river. I couldn't see or hear anything, except the gushing sound of water. I have no recollection what others were doing. My mind clamped onto a vision of a park warden's station not far away. I didn't even think about jumping into the car to drive there. Barefoot, I ran through the woods, creating my own path as I hurdled fallen trees and cleared boughs with my arms flaying, sweeping away whatever was in my way. Even though I didn't really know where I was going in the forest, somehow I reached the station just as a warden was leaving in his truck. Breathless, I cried out, "Help! Help! Leah's missing!"

Leah drowned. About two hours after she was discovered missing, she was found by a search party of kayakers in the shallow water along the shore of the Athabasca River. The Maligne River, which she would have gone in innocence to greet, rose to meet her. It swept her away from us and out to the confluence where the Maligne joins the Athabasca.

Two days later, I lay in the dark, even though day had come like any other day. I could not surface from my bed. How was I going to rise to be a loving mother to my two children, Tekarra and James, and be a wife, daughter, sister, and friend? In the gloomy well of deepest despair, tossing and turning between the crumpled sheets, I prayed. I cried for help like never, *ever* before. Within mere seconds, it felt like I was plugged in. There was an electrical current charging through my body, and it brought a sensation of relief while carrying an indescribable knowingness that penetrated my heart. These few words echoed in my ears:

> This was Leah's destiny, as it is yours and your family's. You are being given the strength and courage to carry on.

I rose. Into the living room where family was grieving, I shuffled, and slowly, with utter conviction, I said, "I have something to tell you."

MOTHER AND BABE 1

Mother and Babe 1 (1986)

After painting "Electrogenesis," I began the next one with a study, a thumbnail sketch. I used a photograph I'd taken of a friend's sister nursing her baby as a reference.

It was at my friend's wedding dinner where I observed them. Baby bound in the safety and comfort of Mother's arms, nursing, while Mother surrendered herself with a calm, supportive arm, a relaxed hand, and eyes glazed to the needs of her babe. There was this palatable bond between the two that was penetrating the space I was sharing with them. I could not comprehend or know it as a single, childless woman.

Three years after making this sketch, that day arrived, and I quickly understood. On August 24, 1989, I gave birth to my first baby, a girl named Tekarra Grace Brown.

Journal Excerpt from August 30, 1989

And suddenly our world changed. I can't think of life without her now. What a miracle. Life. I look at her in amazement that she is the product of the love Norman and I share, our union, and nine months of growth inside my body. She's beautiful …

My emotions are raw as I find tears welling easily to my eyes. This morning was an example. They are tears of the love I feel as the life cycle completes itself from having a mother and being a daughter to having a daughter and being a mother.

Close to twenty-one months after Tekarra's birth, there was another great expectation.

Journal Excerpt from May 22, 1991

Your father and I are getting very anxious to meet you, new one. We have waited and loved you as you grew from a zygote to a fetus and soon-to-be babe in arms … Who are you, little one? What will you look like? What will you be like? Whoever you are, we will help you to blossom, little soul of your own. Your father and I will try to be the guiding spirits you have chosen us for.

Until we meet face-to-face, breast-to-mouth, rest, dear one, for your difficult journey from my womb to my arms.

James David Douglas Brown, our son and second baby, was born on May 27, 1991.

Surprise! It was unexpected, to say the least, when Norman, my husband and father of Tekarra and James, and I found out we were pregnant with our third baby. We were on a weekend ski holiday and had left the children with my mom and dad. I had sensed changes in my body earlier in the week, and the boxed early-pregnancy test we had purchased from the drugstore on the way up to the mountain confirmed my suspicion. In a mixture of gleeful shock, I broke the news to Norman, who was sitting stunned on the bed in the hotel room. We'd been considering more permanent birth control measures and had even taken the step to have a consultation with the doctor on the procedure. The second appointment wasn't made soon enough. Now here we were pregnant.

While Norman was struggling for over a good month, both internally and externally, with the fact that we were going to have another baby and all the implications that meant, my feelings were immediately the opposite.

Journal Excerpt from March 30, 1993 (Five Days after We Discovered I Was Pregnant)

> I can't help but feel the same internal unspoken joy of knowing I'm growing a life inside my body as the first time with Tekarra. How can one describe the presence of life as anything but a miracle? A woman is blessed. Our bodies are sacred places—secure, safe, warm. We give ourselves so that another being may be born into this world …
>
> Yes, new baby of ours, you weren't planned, but you are truly wanted as much as your sister and brother were … I know that having you, new baby, in our lives, really, truly means giving our trust and life to God. Especially, when we start to think more of our own personal desires and then we hit an icy headwall, like we did skiing on the Putnam Station side of Silver Star Mountain.
>
> Please, I ask for your help, dear God, in this writing, which is also like a prayer, to give me the strength and courage to face what you have given and that which you take away. Amen.

I was in love with this baby growing inside me and had faith that Norman was going to adjust, given time, to our growing family. Only heaven knows what possessed me to ask God for help in dealing with what is *given and taken away* in the form of a written prayer at the end of this journal passage, where I am writing about my joy of having our third baby.

Journal Excerpt from November 20, 1993

Well, little one, our sojourn as one body is coming to an end. When is your day? I couldn't sleep that well last night, so when I awoke a 5:30 a.m., I thought, *Might as well shower and enjoy a quiet cup of coffee while writing to you!*

Our fourth season as managers of Tekarra Lodge is over. Tekarra and James went to daycare this season and it worked out well. They were happy, although the best place for them is home with Mom. We ended our "best" season yet with a family Thanksgiving gathering at Tekarrra Lodge. All who came thoroughly enjoyed themselves; the weather was perfect. It was a wonderful feeling to give the time and place to the folks who make up our extended family. We are the very fortunate.

Oh babe, this is your special letter, and I am drawn to think about how beauty can exist with the strife and torment of other lives and circumstances on our planet.

I have loved you and prayed for your growth and health during the past thirty-eight weeks. And now we are all waiting in anticipation to meet you. We don't know if you are Leah Marie or Cameron Norris. It doesn't matter. Just be healthy, babe.

Reading the paper before bed last night left me raw. How can we help the children? You are the most innocent, precious treasures we have. The news is full of stories of injustice, pain, and tragic events. Children are our hope, our future. Didn't Jesus say we must be "like children," unassuming, present, and all-encompassing. The only peace, love, and harmony we can give you are in our home and hopefully, God willing, in your heart. Your communion and relationship with God, the Creator, is paramount. We trust through faith we can guide you to the light of the universe so that you may walk as a beacon to those in need. Our family, in what small way we can, must bring peace and joy to others.

You are our last baby, little one. Tekarra, just over four years old, and James, two and a half years old, are so excited about your arrival and love you already. We have a busy life as managers of Tekarra Lodge. It is our home, our way of life. It is a good and satisfying one. Your father and I will give you the best of ourselves. I want to lead you to your relationship with God and give you the gift of yourself: confidence, independence, compassion, life! A full *life!* Be safe. We are awaiting your coming to the world.

Leah Marie was born on December 1, 1993. Leah Marie died on June 12, 1995. This journal entry, in the form of a letter to her, was enclosed in her funeral card. She never got to read to it. Leah came to this world. She didn't stay long, while I remain.

MOTHER AND BABE 2

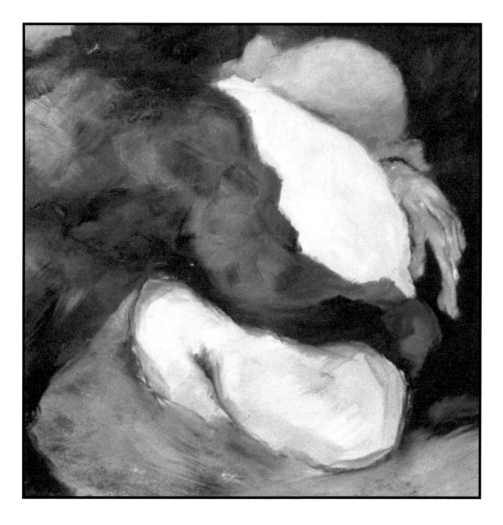

Mother and Babe 2 (1986)

Memory can be a curious thing. I don't remember when I made the painting "Mother and Babe 2," after making the graphite study on paper of a mother nursing her baby, or what I was thinking or not thinking about while painting; however, I do remember how (like when I was painting "Electrogenesis") I allowed myself to *let go* in the process and trust my *intuition* and how I *felt* about what appeared on the canvas through my brush.

There's a dark form resembling a figure that hovers over the abstracted shapes of the baby's body. The mother's lap is indistinguishable. It's a sweeping sea of scumbled brush marks; the mother's limp hand is no contest for the grasp that the weighty arm and pawlike hand of the figure has over the babe. Where did *it* come from? Taking over the picture plane, it gives the impression that *it* may be trying to snatch the baby away from its mother.

This painting, made in art class in 1986, was eerie and disturbing. I destroyed it. Before doing so though, I documented it on slide film (predigital days) for my portfolio.

Early in the morning on June 12, 1995, I came into my office at Tekarra Lodge and was talking with our guest receptionist. We were both mothers and had young children at home. I can't recall how the conversation started, although I do remember matter-of-factly commenting, "I've nursed Leah the longest. I felt I had to keep her the closest to me."

Little did I realize that ten hours later, at approximately 6 p.m., my nursing baby, Leah, would be gone. That day, she went the farthest away from me that she ever could.

It was a Monday, and my to-do list was full. I needed to make a trip into Jasper to do some banking, drive to Hinton where I planned to pick up supplies for the business and groceries for the family, and for the early evening, a family picnic with friends was being organized by our nanny.

Just as I came out of the bank, I ran into a friend and learned that there'd been a tragic car accident on the weekend and a longtime Jasper family lost their twenty-nine-year-old son. So devastating! Jasper is a tight-knit community; a loss of one of its own impacts many, many people.

On my solo, one-hour drive to Hinton, I sent loving thoughts to this family, especially the parents, and at the same time, I filled with deep sadness. I was pondering the question "How do parents who lose a child, no matter what age, go on living?" My mind wandered to memories of my departed grandparents: my father's mother, Faith, whom I never got to meet, and my father's father, Wilson, whom I fortunately got to know and spend some time with. I had been asked by our family to give the eulogy for him at his funeral. I was calling upon my ancestors—bringing them back to life—by remembering, by thinking about them, their lives, and my relationship to them.

Once I arrived in Hinton, I was preoccupied with errands. It wasn't until I was on my way back, home traveling in the car, where my thoughts were more fluid, that I started sifting through the morning news of loss. These thoughts melded into thoughts of *I wonder what's going to happen now.* We were in the early period of the operating season, our fifth year as managers at Tekarra Lodge. We had a nanny at home where we lived on the Tekarra Lodge property to help us care for our three healthy and happy children under five years of age; we hired what we considered to be a great team of staff. I had squeezed out a little time between family and work and was beginning to feel the creative urge. Just a few weeks prior, even though they hadn't been used in more than five years, I had dug out my crusty paintbrushes and oil paints and made a painting outdoors on our deck. I was feeling the promise of spring. Things in our lives were calm and flowing smoothly, but still I was pondering. As experience was my best teacher, I learned that at the lodge, as in life, anything can happen. Someone might quit, the industrial washing machine might break down, a plumbing problem might occur—it could be any number of things on an outlying property with forty-two semirustic cabins and ten lodge rooms or with the guests who booked to stay in these accommodations.

With bags full of groceries from my Hinton shopping trip on my forearms, I leaned my body into the door, turned the knob, and entered our home to see Jacqui, our nanny, washing dishes at the kitchen sink. Leah must have heard my voice. She scampered down the hall, into the kitchen past Jacqui, and was waddling straight toward me. I plopped the grocery bags on the lino and opened my arms wide to embrace her. What struck me instantly was the expression in her eyes and how her cherubic face shone. It was as if she were being lit up from the inside out, in a way I'd never witnessed before. It was intense. It was the way a baby or a very young child might appear when they first wake peacefully up from sleep. Present, with glossy eyes that read, "I've been someplace that you may have forgotten or lost touch with."

I asked Jacqui, "Did Leah just wake up?"

"No," Jacqui assured me. "She's been up for a while. I've changed and fed her. She's been playing."

First, I lost myself when she peered right into me, which was so startling it felt like my heart almost stopped. Then, when I lifted her up and held her close and tight, heart to heart, there was an unusually powerful connection between our bodies, an experience unto itself that my body knew but that my mind was unable to fully decipher.

In the aftermath, during my first year of grieving Leah's death, I read in Dr. Elizabeth Kubler-Ross's book titled *On Children and Death: How Children and Parents Can and Do Cope With Death* that there are a number of recorded instances where young children and teens have said or done things, even leaving notes and drawing pictures, that portend their departure from this world.

What did Leah know? What was she trying to tell me at one and a half years old? She was unable to verbally articulate.

$\mathcal{I}$NNER LANDSCAPES

Inner Landscapes 1 and 2 (1985)

The route was hard to find when dust fogged her rose-colored glasses. It was clear … black panes.

In the aftermath, after *the fact,* there was no turning back. We could not go back in time and change what had happened. Leah, as we knew her to be, wasn't returning. *What if, what if, what if* did not exist. If you've experienced loss of a loved one (or loved ones), you may know how the mind whirls and grapples to configure and reconfigure thoughts, words, and things to come to grasp with reality. You repeat scenarios and say things repeatedly, as if doing this will somehow, miraculously, change the outcome. It's visceral.

Journal Excerpt from June 25, 1995

Leah, where are you? You should be here with us! My heart aches to hold you, kiss you, smell you, hear your laughter, see your smiling face … It's been thirteen days since you've left us, yet I see and feel you so clearly in my mind's eye and heart.

My world without you came crashing down as we arrived on Salt Spring Island, and now as we leave, I sense the same dread as life begins without you.

Never have I felt such an utter sense of complete loss. Please, please forgive me for not being there for you—when you needed me most.

I wished it would have been me. I would have traded places with Leah—or Tekarra or James if it had been either of them. All I knew was life before *the fact;* I didn't know how I was going to continue living after *the fact.* Through my grief and despair, I wrote. A friend had given me *The Artist's Way,* a book by Julia Cameron, where my morning pages of free-flow writing, which is a daily ritual of writing first thing in the morning after waking to stimulate the subconscious, helped me uncover the idea that I wanted and needed to commemorate Leah's life in an art exhibition. I knew there were the artworks I had made years before she was born in art school that related to a toddler in the water and a nursing mother, and a few other paintings I had made after art school. In addition, there were also a few recent artworks that I had made coming to terms with her death, processing my grief. It was while this vision of an exhibition was taking shape in my imagination, though I hadn't discussed it with anyone else or sought out a venue, that I found the two inner landscape drawings. Completely forgotten about, I found them in a portfolio that contained my student drawings. I experienced an immediate jolt of recognition and realization. I now knew what they meant to me.

When I pulled the two drawings with text out of my portfolio, the winds of time lifted me up and away and blew me back to my past. There I was ten years earlier, standing, hunched over the brown, melamine drawing table in art class in university as I prepared to begin working into the two blank sheets of white paper with my graphite sticks and pencils. It was in one complete session and in quite the fury of activity that these drawings were released, for lack of a better way to describe how they came out. There was no photographic image or picture to use for a source. It was almost as if I was translating. The images came first, and then came the text on each drawing.

I was attending the University of Victoria in Victoria, British Columbia. Victoria is on the southern tip of Vancouver Island, where the Pacific Ocean laps at its rocky shoreline and where lush plant and floral life thrive abundantly in the temperate climate. I loved the ease of life in cultured Victoria as it didn't have the population and hustle of its neighboring city, Vancouver, across the Georgia Straight. I rode my bicycle and Honda 90 motorcycle through the winter, without too much concern for heavy traffic, snow, or treacherous mountain roads, as mountains were nowhere in sight.

In this class that day in 1985, I was propelled to make a drawing with a full moon in a dark sky, with a mountain scape featuring a pyramid-shaped peak, with a roadlike map in the foreground, with (what I called) energy lines forking up from the earth to connect and curve over the moon before bouncing off into the night sky represented by expressive marks. Then I added text that read, "The route was hard to find when dust fogged her rose-colored glasses." (I tended to have a Pollyanna view of the world and naivety at twenty-five years of age.)

In the second drawing, I made the road and energy lines within it drift off into the ebony scrawl of graphite marks and wrote the words "It was clear … black panes." I remember feeling like I was trying to see through a windowpane and, while I couldn't quite make out what I was seeing, it was clear that it was black panes—as in black *pains*. Without having any distinct knowledge for the basis or reason for these drawings, I tucked them away into my large, zippered portfolio case.

When we got word that Leah had been found in the Athabasca River, two hours after she went missing, we were at the park warden station. The place I had dashed through the woods to find so we could get help. Friends had learned that we were there and had driven out to pick us up to take us to the hospital, where the search party was delivering Leah's body. In our friend's van on the back seat, Norman and I huddled and sobbed and wrapped in each other's arms.

Unbelievable. It was just the night before we had been driving home from Prince George, where we had gone for the weekend to visit family. I had looked out the car window, while our three young children peacefully slept in their car seats in the back of our silver Subaru, and made note of what looked like a full moon on the rise. Once home, after the kids were in bed, I went to look on the calendar to see if it was a full moon. I was thinking, *Strange things happen on a full moon*. I discovered the moon would be full the next evening on June 12.

Now it was the next evening. Leah was lost and then found drowned. Totally broken, feeling like chunks of me were spewed all over the place, I raised my head out of Norman's embrace and lifted my eyes to see out the back window of the van to behold the brilliant full moon over the Colin Range. The Colin Range is a series of mountain peaks northeast of the town of Jasper in Jasper National Park, with the most impressive of them being Mt. Colin, the limestone peak that is shaped like a pyramid.

I gasped, and then with a forceful exhale, I exclaimed, "Look, Norman! Look! Look at the full moon over Mt. Colin!"

The full moon, the pyramid-shaped mountain, the roadlike map, the energy lines, the darkness, the text "The route was hard to find when dust fogged her rose-colored glasses. It was clear … black panes." Seeing through a glass darkly, it was there in the drawings executed in 1985, though not understood at that time. It was *seeing through a glass darkly* on June 12, 1995. It was the end of time, as I had known it to be.

VIEW FROM THE ROCK GARDENS

View from the Rock Gardens (1988)

Jasper called my name. Victoria gave me time to experience life alongside the Pacific Ocean, but I was a mountain girl at heart. Near the end of studying for my bachelor of fine arts degree, I was unsure of my direction. I had never been much of an advance planner. Rather, I was more prone to listen to my inner voice—to where I was directed to go or what I needed to do. (Needless to say, this method of making decisions raised a few eyebrows, though those who knew me would shake their heads when my life decisions fell into place after it first appeared to be rash and chaotic.) Indeed, that was the case when I first arrived in Victoria.

On the ferry crossing over to Victoria in early September, I was in a reverie seeing myself in the fine arts program; however, my mind brought me back to reality thinking it was time, at twenty-four years old, to be practical. I had a combined total of three years of college and university, at different institutions behind me, and an array of various subjects that I had explored because my interests spanned many disciplines. It seemed like teaching was a solid choice and would give me a career to focus on, alongside helping young people. I had been accepted into the teachers program.

On registration day at the university, rather than going to the education desk to complete course registration, I wandered over to the fine arts desk and signed up for courses. I didn't have a portfolio with me; nevertheless, I had taken a few fine art courses in the previous year and loved drawing and making things, even as a little girl. That afternoon when I arrived home after registration, I was so thrilled and overjoyed that I had done this and that I had gotten in without a portfolio. However, by morning, that excitement had transformed into fear. I needed to think about my future and student loans. My education was my responsibility. How would I make a living as an artist? What had I done?

The following day, rather than go unregister for the fine art courses I signed up for, I went back to the university to register into the courses I was required to take in the education department. For five weeks, I attended the teacher training courses. On Thanksgiving weekend 1984, I wasn't feeling at all thankful. Jogging was one of my passions. Through Beacon Hill Park with its profusion of autumn glory in the dribbling rain, I trotted, feeling wet and upset. I stopped to rest on the embankment overlooking the rise and fall of the gray-green ocean waves crashing onto the pebbly beach. As I internally questioned myself while peering out to the distant horizon, I felt like I was one of those waves swelling to the point they had to break. And I did. A wail of tears welled up and was released when I asked myself what I really wanted and where I wanted to be. When classes resumed on Tuesday after the holiday weekend, I marched over to the fine arts building to speak with the chairman of the department and told him how I had made a mistake.

In his authoritative tone, he said, "Destanne Norris, we were wondering where you were. Get in here."

With commitment and dedication, I made up the work that I had missed in my art classes during the first six weeks of the semester and at the end of the school year was surprised and honored with a fine arts bursary.

Three years later, after graduation with my honors degree in fine arts, it was time to leave Victoria for my next adventure. Unsure, of how I was going to make my living as a freshly graduated artist, I applied for a six-week French immersion program in Quebec and was accepted. With a couple months to spare before flying to Quebec, I decided to venture in my trusty and a little rusty Dodge cargo van to the Rocky Mountains. Driving into Banff National Park, I saw the directional road sign for Jasper. Jasper. I liked the way that word sounded as it rolled around on my tongue and thought, *Cool name. I'd like to go there someday.*

With a little time to spare, I picked up a temporary job at a seasonal cabin resort in Banff National Park. That's where we met over coffee that I was serving. He had a slight but muscular build, dark hair with a high forehead and cheekbones, a straight nose, and piercing blue eyes behind his glasses that smiled like his lips. Norman was his name, and he was working with a construction crew building new Pan Abode cabins. We spent a little time getting to know each other after work: talking, eating together, running, bicycling, including an introductory rock-climbing lesson as Norman was a climber, a mountain man. It felt easy and natural to be with him, but then I had to leave. Norman said I should consider coming to Jasper, where he lived, when I came back from Quebec. I was at my parents' place, my home base, preparing for my upcoming trip when the phone rang.

It was Norman. In his quiet, soft voice that was sure of itself even through the nerves, he stated, "I have arranged some time off work. Don't go. I am coming to see you."

Norman drove six hours to see me. It was a two-week whirlwind courtship. Before he left to go back to work, while we had stopped to rest from bicycling amid sun-dappled poplar trees whose leaves were shimmering in the breeze, he asked "Will you marry me?" Totally unsuspecting, I took a second to answer. "Yes!" I exclaimed. I moved to Jasper, never studied French in Quebec, and married him six months later on New Year's Eve 1987.

A new year, a new beginning. Jasper became home. Norman was born and raised in Jasper to a loving, close-knit family, much like my own. We shared similar values, morals, love for each other, and the outdoor life. Importantly, he knew about my passion and supported my dream of being an artist. During our first year of married life, during days off from work, we went on many excursions into mountain wilderness areas. Since I also had a passion for sports, physical activity, and trying new things, Norman had no challenge encouraging me to learn how to rock climb.

The painting "View from the Rock Gardens" was a memorial to my first sport climb on a bolted route at the Rock Gardens, a popular crag to the east of where the Maligne River snakes its way through the predominantly limestone Maligne Canyon. Norman had taken a photograph of me in a lotus position as I meditated upon my most recent accomplishment of scaling one of the routes on this rocky cliff with ropes and rubber-toed slippers. The spectacular vista was the Athabasca River coursing through the valley close to the mountains that flank it on either side. I made a drawing from the photograph, then the oil painting, which hung in our home.

It would be seven years later that Leah would fall into the Maligne River, while we were picnicking at the Sixth Bridge, and be carried out into the Athabasca River, to be discovered in a shallow eddy that could be seen from the *view from the Rock Gardens*.

Moments in Time

Moments in Time 1 and 2 (1995)

Norman and I didn't wait too long after we were married to begin our family. Within four years of our first baby being born, we had three children: Tekarra, James, and Leah. They meant the world to us. Our lives revolved around raising our children the best way we knew how and spending as much time as possible with them between our work schedules. It was our good fortune that our employment as managers at Tekarra Lodge gave us flexibility; we were dedicated to the lodge, where we also lived on the property. It was more than a job; it was our home.

Given our work, the children were growing up with exposure to lots of people. Bubbly Tekarra attracted kids and adults alike to her with her talkative, outgoing nature; observant James was quieter and reserved in his behavior, yet we watched similar actions, especially with other kids, who would gravitate toward him and want to touch his golden-white hair. Tekarra and James were the best of friends as siblings and welcomed their baby sister, Leah, into their circle with open arms. Leah was a mere two weeks old when she first smiled. I witnessed her smile when she and I, as a nursing pair, were on the bed lounging in our pajamas after Norman, Tekarra, and James had left to go skiing for the day in mid-December. Leah seemed extremely alert and aware, and as she grew into her personality more, she had quite a presence. An acquaintance saw Leah at seventeen months of age and commented that she recognized a leader in Leah. There was rarely a disagreement or fight among our three happy and, for the most part, healthy young children. We had won the lottery.

Most of our travel with our young children was to my parents' and extended families' homes in the Shuswap and North Okanagan regions in British Columbia. We spent considerable time in Jasper with Norman's family, who were very supportive and helped us care for our children, but we went as often as we could to visit my family. June 12, 1995, was a Monday, and it was on the Friday before this day that we decided to go for a weekend getaway to visit Norman's cousin and wife who lived south of Prince George on a ranch near the Fraser River. We arrived on Friday evening, and Saturday, we explored and played outside with the kids after visiting in the morning. Norman had Leah in the backpack, while Tekarra and James were running around him as he flew a kite in the lower field beside the river. (All the while, Norman told me later, Leah stood on the metal sides of the backpack, using her legs to bounce up and down. She wanted out and off his back to be free to run around to play with her siblings.)

I perched on the hillside above the expanse of farmland to watch and sketch them with pen and watercolor in my sketch book. Feeling somewhat weary, it felt good to have a little time out to just observe them scamper in the grass and then try to capture these fleeting *moments in time* visually. The first sketch I made was of my family flying the kite, and in the second sketch, I zoomed in for a close-up of the Fraser River, even though I was quite a distance away and didn't have binoculars. It was the river that caught my attention. Water was on my mind.

Before settling into bed the night we arrived, I perused the bookshelf in the bedroom we were sleeping in at Norman's cousin's home. The book that caught my attention was written a year after the *Titanic* sank and had excerpts from people who had survived. While Leah, who was between us in bed, and Noman slept, I dived into this book and could not stop reading these true accounts of this historic tragedy at sea. It was the same on the following night; all was quiet in the house and as everyone slept undisturbed, with the bedside lamp shedding low light for me to read by, I flipped through the pages. Transported back to the event and immersed in these true stories through the survivors' senses and their descriptions, it was as if I was living it. Into the early morning hours, I continued to absorb more and more until I was saturated and could no longer do so. Drowning. Death by water.

Despite feeling a little preoccupied after my late-night reading frenzy and its impact on my thoughts, we all had a wonderful weekend visiting, playing, and relaxing. On Sunday afternoon, our contented family of five traveled back to Jasper. For some unusual reason, I had a peacock feather in the car. Turning to admire and revel in the beautiful image that filled my heart, our three young children tucked in beside each other safely in their car seats on the back seat, I dubbed each of them, with this iridescent peacock feather in my hand, to be princesses and a prince—to live a full and happy life. Unaware that in less than twenty-four hours, one of our princesses would leave us.

Why Leah? Why me? Why us? Why, why, why—a powerful word. Questions. No answers. Totally out of the blue, a few weeks prior to Leah's passing, I had asked Tracy, our guest receptionist, "Why do bad things happen to good people?" We were good people. My parents drove through the night to come be with us in Jasper once they learned the news and heard my cry of desperation on the telephone. In the early morning hours, we were all grieving in the living room. I was wrapped in my dad's arms on the sofa (he had always been my philosopher to talk and muse over ideas with) and wailed, "Why, Dad? Why Leah? Why me?" In his most loving, calm voice, my grieving father responded, "Why not you?"

Oh, my heart, my heart. It was if his profound answer sliced one of my arteries. I needed to comprehend the wisdom between his words, and when I did, a few minutes later, I knew. As much as he loved me, and no matter how I or we as a family thought we had been good people and didn't deserve this (who does deserve this?), tragedy strikes. Death is part of life. *It* happens. No one is spared. A kite fluttering in the breeze, a feather afloat on the surface of water, we have but *moments in time*.

AWAKENING AT THE SITE

Awakening at the Site (1995)

The park warden whom I met just leaving the station after I darted through the woods to find help drove me back to the location while calling in others to help in the search for Leah. I was oblivious to what others were doing when we got back there. I do know I ended up on the ground, flailing and wailing, "I should have known. I should have been able to stop this. I created this." The park warden who hovered over me and was trying to ask me questions, I am sure, was totally confused and mystified by what he was hearing. The visions of paintings I had made, things I had thought, said, and done, played like a fast-forwarding film on the screen of my mind.

I had been so anxious two hours earlier when I returned home after my shopping trip to Hinton and my embrace with Leah. Our nanny's friends who were doing most of the organizing had come, shortly thereafter, to drive the children and Jacqui to the picnic site before Norman and I were ready to leave work. I could hardly contain my energy, wondering if I should run the five-mile distance there to help dissipate my anxiousness, my nervous energy that I could not understand. We decided we'd make the drive over together in our car with Kona, our gentle, black Labrador.

When we arrived, Tekarra, James, and Leah came running up to greet us for their usual hugs as they did when we'd been apart, even if we'd been gone only for short while. They were the only children present. The scene was serene: the children playing around the picnic area, our nanny and the other adults watching the children, placing food to share on the table. I gathered Leah in my arms and strolled over to another picnic table, a short distance away, laid a blanket down, talked to her, and blew on her belly while I changed her diaper. Norman was with us; he admired his beautiful daughter looking over my shoulder.

At a year and a half, she didn't speak much, yet she watched. She seemed to know things.

Once Leah's diaper was changed, Norman went to tie Kona to a tree and Leah was standing at his feet. I was famished. With all that had transpired that day, I hadn't eaten much, and I needed to get some food in me as I was getting shaky.

I called over to Norman and asked, "Shall I put Leah in the backpack?"

The often-used blue child carrier backpack was propped up beside me, ready for her to be lowered into and to be safely anchored to me on my back. I didn't wait for an answer. She was safe with her dad. He was watching her, I thought. I went to collect a plate of food and proceeded to sit down in a lawn chair. That was when, before glancing up, I felt the demanding urge and called out, "Where's Leah?" Then I saw everyone's heads swivel back and forth, eyes wide-open. I saw everyone but Leah. My madness had begun.

Lying in the dirt in the fetal position, as my mind was processing that Leah had most likely transitioned from this planet through the water, it was if an unconscious part of my body awakened to birth her death. Groans and moans were guttural. I was a wild animal. Every fiber, cell in my body was exploding. I was overcome with such strong expulsion sensations in my uterus. They were laborlike contractions.

"Awakening at the Site," a self-portrait, was painted six months later as a visual expression of my madness, angst, and helplessness, to be able to reach beyond the edge and bring Leah back from the rushing water, to earth, to breath, to life. The only way that I was going to move through this excruciating pain was to be present with it. The future did not exist; it was only ever now.

The morning after, as family all came together at our home, I was acutely aware of my overpowering yearning to see Leah again, to hold her, to smell her, to bring her home to be with all of us one last time. She was at the hospital, where she had been taken after being found in an eddy along the Athabasca riverbank and where Norman and I had gone to view her body. Guided by my consuming sensation and thoughts, I phoned the hospital and asked if we could come get Leah. Only to be told that this was unusual and that since they'd never had this request, they needed to consult with a doctor first. Our wait was not long. The phone rang. Our request was granted. We could come get Leah on the condition that we'd bring her back to the hospital in a couple hours. In an instant, Norman and I hopped into our car to bring the body of our bundled baby girl home.

Long Mornings

Long Mornings (1996)

I was extremely grateful to the doctor at the hospital who allowed us to bring Leah's body home from the hospital. All the family had time to hold, be with her, and say good-bye. It was also important for Jacqui, our nanny from the Philippines, to have some time with Leah. The Filipino mourning traditions are quite different from typical North American traditions. In the Philippines, the body of the deceased is prepared, dressed up, often with makeup, and placed in an open casket for a wake and late-night vigil to honor the deceased. Jacqui had told me when we had been discussing funeral rites, before Leah left us, that some people will even sleep with the deceased body of their loved one. The Filipino way of showing love and respect to their deceased by holding vigil, it seemed to me, is more natural, healthy, and healing than our rituals, acknowledging the cycle of life and death by giving those mourning time to say good-bye. They don't keep death separate and distant, behind closed doors.

Though I listened to what I was called to do, I did keep Leah's bedroom door in our home closed for a long time afterward. Her scent, which lingered in her room, would bring me to my knees and make me incapable of functioning. This yearning to have her back was persistent, never leaving day and night. How we craved to have *long mornings* with Leah again, like I titled this pencil sketch of Leah with her dad, like we did with all three of our children.

Norman was devastated losing Leah and grieved her like only he could, certainly more internally and privately than me. He was always reluctant and apprehensive about how I expressed my thoughts and feelings so openly. As well, he was somewhat challenged by my preoccupation with the metaphysical and spiritual. However, there were a couple instances involving Leah that made him really question and consider these things.

The first instance he told me about was after Leah's passing. He admitted that when I was changing her diaper at the picnic site and he peered over my shoulder, lovingly focused on her, the way she looked into him startled and rattled him, similar to what I experienced with her a couple hours earlier when I returned home from my shopping trip. If eyes are windows to our souls, what was she trying to communicate to both of us?

Although Leah was not talking, she was making plenty of sounds. In early spring, one of the things she loved to do when she was out on the deck with us, where our property was surrounded by the evergreen forest, was to lift her head back and cry "Caw, caw, caw." She was imitating the ravens that flew around the property and hung out in the treetops at Tekarra Lodge. We thought her so amusing, our little toddler lifting her head, stretching her voice, beckoning, and singing to these birds. It was not long after her passing that the second instance came when Norman and I were awakened before dawn one morning by a congress of ravens squawking and screeching to us outside our bedroom window. We both looked at each other and knew what each other was thinking: *Leah.*

Journal Excerpt from June 26, 1995 (Written While We Were on Salt Spring Island, Where We Had Traveled to Heal)

> Oh my little Lea-Lea. My little songbird. What sweet pleasures you gave to me. Our lullaby song, our tender moments as a nursing pair. James came to me from the playground where he frolics with Tekarra and Dad.
>
> He said, "You know what Wendy said to Captain Hook? You need a mother very, very badly." Then he reaches up to give me a hug and kiss, before going into the trailer for a cookie. Off he goes to the park.
>
> I'm cold. The sun cannot penetrate my chill. Tekarra drew a picture of you in the sand. We are all trying to reach you, to etch you into our daily lives.
>
> Norman just brought the kids back and a butterfly followed them. Is that you, Leah?

The last picture of Leah was taken on Mother's Day, Sunday, May 14, 1995. With her pink corduroy coat in one hand, she stood grounded, waiting to go. With her ruby lips slightly parted and her bright, brown, round eyes glowing, she stared through the camera lens at me. On her dress is a butterfly.

THE WAY WE WERE

The Way We Were (1995)

Once we returned home from our trip to Salt Spring and Vancouver Island, the realization that we, as a family, could never return to *the way we were* burrowed deeply into my bone marrow. My grief journal became a solace as I allowed my emotions and thoughts in words to ooze out onto the page. It was where I could talk to her.

There was a river of tears that thundered through the ravine of my sleepless nights. I struggled with the mystery, incessantly asking why, feeling betrayed, and trying to find acceptance. I pleaded for answers, knowing full well that they could not and would not be given. I knew I would have to learn to trust and find truth in living through my greatest nightmare, but I didn't know how I was going to do this. Leah was our gift. My gift. And the one she left me was wrapped up in faith, hope, and love.

Journal Excerpt from July 8, 1995

Dear Leah,

I am only beginning to realize that I won't see you again as Leah Marie Brown. The pain is so deep I could burst—have burst. How do I let you go? I guess I want what we had and must face the facts that it will not be.

It's Saturday and we have been home at Tekarra Lodge since Tuesday night. It's hard to be here and resume our lives without you. We all feel it—Dad, Tekarra, and James.

I'm still having trouble coming to terms with why? Why you, why me, why us, and why our family?

I want to write to you. I want you to read what I write about you. I want you to know that your life meant more to me than my own, and if there was any way we could have traded places, I would have given you my life.

I feel the doors that separate us are impenetrable. What are you doing right now? Dancing with the wind? Singing with the angels? How close are you? Do you remember me? Do you know how much love I have for you?

I like to believe you are safe, free from pain and suffering, that you feel love and are giving love, but I truly don't know. Is death birth? Are you living more than you were on this planet? Or are you on this planet only in a different form?

If you are close by, why can't you make contact? Tell me you are okay and that you will meet me again someday.

Do souls know time as we know time in our bodies? Can you see the years to come, or is everything happening at once? That it's all happening *now!*

If our souls are on a journey to learn and experience, where do we stop or begin? Oh heavenly Father, what is your grand plan?

How can I learn and give of myself again when I feel so hurt and broken inside? I need to mend, to lick and nurture my wounds. Norman needs me. Tekarra and James need me. I need to be present for my work at Tekarra Lodge and feel like I am unable to concentrate, focus, or give very much of myself.

If Leah chose us and chose to have a short life as Leah, what's next?

Will I ever gain insight or answers to my many questions, or is this all a test of my faith, trust, and love of God? Belief that there is a purpose, there is a reason, there is meaning in this pain and suffering of having to live without you, Leah Marie?

I pray to you, God. If I can do anything, please help me to live a fuller, better life in memory of Leah.

Journal Excerpt from July 9, 1995

Today I busied myself with earthly things, Leah! I had to. I've let everything slide since we've been home. In no way does it mean that you weren't with me all day.

Last night, my body, heart, and soul ached and longed for you. I cannot accept the fact that you are not here with your family. I realize that I cannot accept it because you are here with us. You will always be part of us, of our family, of who we are and hope to be. I pause and can feel your energy, the spirit of Leah, as we knew her this time. You are such a loving, joyful soul who blessed our lives with so much beauty.

How can we measure your earthly years of one and a half with others? What you gave and gained with your encounter this time was all you obviously needed; otherwise, you would still be here. Somehow, it's Catch-22 for us. We would have preferred to see you live a long earthy life while we were your parents, but we could never possess you in any case. As parents, we must learn to let go. I feel though we have unfinished ties. Is this my dreaming, my desires of holding you in my arms and being your mother? Can I believe in miracles?

Oh dear Heavenly Father, you know I have always "willed to will thy will." I have experienced many trials and tribulations on my path, but this is my most difficult part of the journey. Why me? Why our family? What do you have in store?

Please, I pray, please help me to listen with my heart and soul so that the choices we make are those ordained by you, oh great, all-knowing, all-loving, all-powerful One. I will do my utmost best to hear your voice in the wind! Amen.

Journal Excerpt from July 21, 1995

Leah, you were our true gift! On Saturday night after I wrote this last passage, I dealt with the issue of betrayal. As I tucked myself under the down comforter in the tent, I wrestled with the feelings of betrayal. How hard I have tried to love, be compassionate, be thoughtful, and place my children and husband as the focus of my life. And then, for you, dear Leah, to be taken from us so suddenly.

I guess I was trying to work through the "Why me? Why us?" syndrome. Why do we have to experience so much pain and suffering being left here without you when all I've tried to do is be a good person. My mind said, "Betrayed." However, I've worked through those thoughts and feelings and have come full circle to my heart of hearts knowing. This is that I/we will never know why or can explain why you were taken from us.

Journal Excerpt from July 24, 1995

Oh Leah, my darling, my love … I sobbed to your dad last night that it was not fair. We were left behind. What is time though?

I cannot make any predictions or theorize about what is happening, where you are, how we are doing. We just have to live it moment to moment, breath to breath. Whatever. You are here now with me.

Lovingly supportive in my human quest to put some meaning into what we on this planet have problems comprehending. We think we need to plan, direct, know. Funny how it all takes place regardless. Trust, trust, trust. Faith, hope, and love. Yet the greatest of these is *love*.

Journal Excerpt from October 5, 1995

My darling, the leaves are falling off the trees, the days are crisp and cool, and you cannot see or feel this. The shock, numbness, and disbelief have passed. Now day to day, hour to hour, breath to breath, we live with your memory.

I was trying to imagine the very beginning of our development. That spark of life is our mystery. And Leah, so is your passing on and into another dimension, world, state, form, beginning—which is it? All of these, one, or none?

What is true? The only truth I know is that night turns to day (and will shortly), the trees are losing their leaves, the bull elk bugles agitated and anxious in full rut, the air is permeated with change. I see autumn as preparation for the stillness of winter just as spring ushers in the growth of summer. These are truths. And so are you, Leah!

Whatever form you have now or existence you lead, you are my truth.

You came to us, through us, but not from us. We watched you grow in love. We are continuing (or attempting to continue) to live without you as our baby, only as a memory, as a truth.

Journal Excerpt from November 22, 1995

My breath was being squeezed out of me as I closed my eyes and rested on my pillow. Where are you, Leah? You are more—greater—than my memory.

The ache and pain of your physical absence from our lives falls over me sometimes. It jumps out unexpectedly. I choke. I lose myself in your memory, clawing at any way to bring you back. Knowing, oh knowing, the impossibility of it happening.

We have carried on with our day-to-day activities. Tekarra and James are doing wonderfully well. Thank heavens for their laughter and play.

Well, baby Leah, I wrote to you before your birth. I never *ever* believed two years later I would be writing to you after your death. That word is difficult for me. *Death. Drowning.* I like *passing on* much better. *Death* sounds final. *Drowning* sounds cold. *Passing on* is transformation. Your body to ashes drifting out to sea, your spirit eternally with me. And elsewhere. I can only imagine.

Help me, please, to open my heart and eyes to my truths, Leah, spirit child of mine. Keep me mindful and in tune.

The river. We went back to the Maligne River, two months after Leah's funeral, to give her back to the water that took her away. In an intimate family ceremony at the same picnic site, we formed a circle and I used her baptismal candle to light the royal purple candle being cupped by each person present. With our candlelight shining, Jacqui strummed her guitar and softly sang the "Spirit Song." I read a passage "On Children" from the book *The Prophet* by Kahlil Gibran. We prayed. We silently held space. We remembered. We went to the riverbank, gently tipped the urn enclosing her ashes, and let the remains of her body float away in the river toward the eternal sea.

There is an engraved, flat, gray, granite marker that lies in the verdant grass at the Jasper Cemetery for Leah with an epitaph under her name and dates of her birth and death that reads, "A Free Spirit." Gracing each of the corners of the marker is the engraved image of a butterfly.

Iris

Iris (1996)

L eah wore her butterfly dress, that she wore on Mother's Day, for her funeral. It was held at 2:00 p.m. on Thursday, June 15, 1995, at the Jasper United Church, three days after she drowned. We arrived at the church to see Leah appearing like she was just peacefully sleeping. She was angel white, so perfect in every way, lying in the pink, satin-lined coffin. We were told by the funeral directors to go sit up in the wooden pews at the front of the church reserved for ourselves and our family. The directors would wheel Leah down the aisle in her coffin after the guests arrived and were seated.

What? I couldn't bear the thought.

I said, with vehemence, "No! I am sorry. I can't do that. I want to be beside her coffin in the vestibule until everyone is here."

The funeral director replied, "We can't let you do that. It'll be too difficult for people to see. It will be too hard for them."

My dad walked over to where the funeral director and I were having this strained discussion. In a controlled yet firm alto voice, he leaned his large-framed body in and said, "If this is what she wants to do, let her do it."

In the vestibule, a chair was placed by her coffin, wherein at Leah's feet we had placed some of her special things: her toy camera, one of her books, a stuffed animal, and blanket. I sat down on the edge of the chair, reached into the coffin, and carefully lifted her soft hand, encircling it in the palm of mine. Norman stood behind me, his hand on my shoulder.

Most people came by us, and when our eyes met, minimal words were uttered or even needed; the expression on their faces and in their eyes said it all. Only a few passed by without turning to look at us. The church became filled to the rafters, leaving some standing in the back.

When it was time for Leah to be trolleyed down in her coffin to the front of the church, and Norman and me to make our way to our waiting seats in the pews, Leah's hand had warmed to body temperature in mine. It was as if, in my imagining, she was present, only with eyes closed, and had somehow, through our connection and touch, been brought back to life.

Although a dense fog of grief swirled around and in me at the funeral, my mind was crystal clear in what I was being directed and given the strength to do. Near the end of her service, I was compelled to speak, to let everyone know the message I'd been given. This was the message that had come in the form of an electrical charge in my body and the voice I'd heard, after I desperately prayed a couple days earlier, when I was not able to surface from my bed or know how I was going to go on living. At the lectern, I shared. I opened my mouth and surrendered to the words and ideas that came through me though they were not of me.

To finish, I opened the message of thanks I'd prepared and read.

> As we struggle to answer the many questions we have over losing our baby Leah, our blessing, our gift, God has given us one answer through you these past couple days and, especially, today.
>
> Our family and friends from the many paths we tread in this life are gathered around us with comfort and love shown through their helping hands, their dedication to our needs through the meals, food, flowers, cards, kind words, thoughts, and prayers.
>
> Our gift to you in return is our deepest, most heartfelt thank-you.
>
> In our loss, we can count one blessing, and that is all of *you*.
>
> May God keep you and your families safe.

I couldn't stay for the tea reception prepared by the ladies in the church to visit with all who came after her funeral was over and her body was driven away by the funeral directors to be cremated. I had no energy left. I had to leave.

I went home to Tekarra Lodge, where I did not notice the Canadian flag in the center of the property flying at half-mast. It had been lowered by two of our staff without me realizing it. Several weeks later, when I mentioned to one of my staff that I wish the flag had been flown at half-mast, I was told it had been lowered for three days. I thought back to earlier in the spring, when I'd looked at our flag fluttering on its pole, and thought, *If anyone we knew would pass away, we would fly the flag at half-mast.*

The support and love from so many people, even those we did not know, came through many ways; we were extremely moved and grateful. Our team of staff was outstanding, as well as the support from the owners of the company we worked for. We were given the opportunity to comfortably take leave from our work, once our out-of-town family had gone home, to travel to Salt Spring and Vancouver Island to begin our healing journey as a family of four. However, the real journey began once we returned to Tekarra Lodge, to our home and work, to resume our forever changed lives.

Once I returned to work, I recall commenting to a colleague, "I've never felt more alive in my grief."

They responded with a surprised and shocked expression. It did sound like a weird and strange thing to feel and even admit to. The emotional pain was so severe it brought my entire sense of *being* in the world sharply focused and tuned into the present moment. Moreover, at an unconscious level, I knew the only way I was going to process this pain that had weight, color, and shape was to surrender to it and allow it to move *through* me in whatever way it chose, whenever and wherever.

People would try and comfort me by saying, "Time heals all wounds." And despite being well-meaning, I couldn't fathom this. I detested this aphorism.

As I learned though, moving through the pain over time, the wound did change form. I spent as much time as possible holding Tekarra and James close to me, trying to be a good mother, playing with them, being with them and Norman after work. Family and friends were there for us but did not smother us. I talked a lot about Leah and what happened; I read a lot of books on death, dying and grieving; I spent time alone and in nature walking and running; I prayed; I meditated; I cried torrents of tears. And there were evenings spent in the first two months where I drank too much wine and smoked cigarettes to help numb my pain, until my body and mind said, *Enough*. I was grateful for my journal writing, drawing, and painting. This became a way for me to transmute the compressed energy ball of hardened black pain into another form, to help release it and set it free. I couldn't bury my feelings. I had to let them flow like a river.

My mind continued to pose endless questions without answers forthcoming. The essential questions revolved around the *mysteries* of our human existence: of our beginnings and endings, our life and death, our destiny, and what lies in between—our past, present, and future.

It was when I finally accepted these questions were unanswerable, that I must live them, that I began to transform on my healing journey. I became aware that I needed to reframe my questions so that I could be open to the possibility of finding answers and discovering a new purpose and meaning. The following were a few of these new questions:

- How could I celebrate and honor Leah's life the best?

- How did I think Leah would want me to go on living?

- What difference could I make in the lives of others, especially my children?

One of the answers to the questions I posed revealed itself to me while writing in my journal ten months later. It was the idea to have an exhibition of my artworks to commemorate and celebrate Leah's brief life. As well, I thought, an exhibition would be a way to give thanks to our family, friends, and community for their support that was beyond expectation, beyond belief. I had no plan in how I was going to accomplish this or where the venue would be. In a series of synchronistic events soon thereafter, Sunrise Galleries in Jasper opened their doors to me, and the exhibition date was set for June 7, 1996, five days short of Leah's first anniversary.

The artworks that I'd made before she was born and those made the first year after she died comprised the exhibition. With each artwork was a card with the title and medium used in making the artwork, the date each piece was made, and a short-written description of how I saw the relationship between the artwork, life, and Leah. On a pamphlet listing the artworks in the exhibition, I wrote,

> My intention is to show the mysterious dance between the past and present. Our earthly existence is shrouded in this mystery. Ultimately, it is not ours to know but to live—to live fullest in the moment—in faith, in hope, in love.

The first artwork in the exhibition was the painting "Electrogenesis," which made some viewers gasp and ask me, "How did you paint Leah into the picture?" because it looked like her.

I responded, "I didn't. That's how I painted this toddler eight years before Leah was born."

The last artwork in the exhibition was a painting I made of a solitary iris. In 1987, I'd taken a weeklong workshop and had been presented with an iris at the end of the course. I never quite understood its meaning or importance when it was given to me. I decided to paint an iris in 1996 because, recalling this flower being gifted to me nine years earlier, I felt it would be the best flower to represent Leah's coming to the world and her departure from it, and the healing journey I was on.

After making the painting, I looked up the meaning of the word *iris* in the dictionary.

IRIS n [L, FR, Gr]: The Greek goddess of the rainbow and a messenger of the gods.

This flower symbolized a message of hope and promise. It couldn't have been more fitting. This definition was on the descriptive card beside the final painting, "Iris." Under the definition, I'd written,

The Healing,

The Mystery,

The Gift of Life continues …

$\mathcal{A}$FTERWORD

After Leah departed and the exhibition was over, I knew, without a doubt, that I was supposed to focus on being as good a mother as I could possibly be to Tekarra and James, wife to Norman, *and* to paint. We finished the 1996 summer season at Tekarra Lodge, and by the spring of 1997, we had left our management positions and home to live in the town of Jasper so I could do just that.

Although my grieving and healing continued to ebb and flow, I felt an intensified sense of purpose. My desire was to love and live more passionately and meaningfully because of Leah *but* especially *for* Tekarra, James, and Norman.

Grieving and healing from loss is like sailing *through* stormy, uncharted seas. We all navigate these waters of life's mysteries in our own boats, in our own unique styles. Notwithstanding, I know that on our voyage, if we allow *grace* to fill our sails and ourselves to feel, to *be* with our pain and sorrow, to take whatever time we need, even if it takes years (it's never too late), we will reach that far shore. Sometimes we need to give ourselves permission to let go and open to our buried treasure trove of memories and to make something, write something, do something in memory and honor of our loved ones. Sometimes we need to put our anchors down and be still, to listen within more, to trust what we know to be true for ourselves and then act upon that truth. Sometimes we simply just need to use our voices.

How do you answer the unanswerable questions you have when someone you love dies? You don't. You can't. The answers we seek are in the questions we've not yet formed.

Use your imagination. Envision your loved one in front of you. They're smiling, and their eyes that emanate with love and light look deeply into your heart and fill it with joy. Imagine what they'd be saying to you. How does that make you feel and think? How would they want you to be living? What would they be encouraging you to do? How would they want you to be remembering them? What difference could you make because of them?

Try reframing your questions. Like me, you may discover new purpose, new meaning, and newfound joy.

The gift is in *the heart of life*.

$\mathcal{A}$CKNOWLEDGMENTS

My heartfelt gratitude and appreciation go to the many people from Jasper and beyond, too numerous to mention by name, but you know who you are. You were there for us in various capacities from the time Leah went missing to her being found and from that time forward, especially during that first year afterward.

I give thanks to my family and Norman's family for their love and support, to Jacqui Naguit, and to many friends who've been there for me, including those who've helped me by listening as I shared my story in conversations and presentations over the years.

I also thank Karen Close, editor of *Sage-ing with Creative Spirit, Grace & Gratitude,* who asked me to write an article for this journal and then encouraged me to write a book, and my readers of the first manuscript, Janet Woods, Christine Pilgrim, Maeribeth Sullivan, Coleen Robb, Sarah Kennedy, and Claudette Bouchard, who gave me valuable feedback and suggestions.

And finally, I thank Tekarra and James, who mean the world to me, and Corky, who walks beside me while holding my hand.

Printed in the United States
By Bookmasters